What Research Says to the Teacher

Vocabulary Knowledge:
Guidelines for Instruction
by Judith L. Irvin

nea PROFESSIONAL LIBRARY
National Education Association
Washington, D.C.

Acknowledgment

Portions of this monograph have been adapted from Judith L. Irvin, *Reading and the Middle School Student: Strategies to Enhance Literacy*. Copyright © 1990 by Allyn and Bacon. Used with permission.

Copyright © 1990
National Education Association of the United States

Printing History
  First Printing: May 1990

Note

The opinions expressed in this publication should not be construed as representing the policy or position of the National Education Association. Materials published by the NEA Professional Library are intended to be discussion documents for educators who are concerned with specialized interests of the profession.

Library of Congress Cataloging-in-Publication Data

Irvin, Judith L., 1947–
  Vocabulary knowledge : guidelines for instruction / by Judith L. Irvin.
  p. cm.—(What research says to the teacher)
  Includes bibliographical references.
  ISBN 0-8106-1085-X
  1. Vocabulary—Study and teaching. I. National Education Association of the United States. II. Title. III. Series.
LB1574.5.I75   1990
372.6'1—dc20   90-32096
                                                                CIP

CONTENTS

INTRODUCTION 5

A REVIEW OF THE RESEARCH 6
   The Importance of Vocabulary Knowledge 6
   Factors in Vocabulary Acquisition 7
      Knowing Words 7
      Context 8
      Definitions 9
      Size and Growth of Vocabulary 10

ISSUES RELATED TO VOCABULARY INSTRUCTION 12
   Choosing Words for Instruction 12
   Elements of Effective Instruction 14

GUIDELINES FOR INSTRUCTION 16

LEARNING STRATEGIES 18
      List-Group-Label-Write 18
      Semantic Feature Analysis 20
      Graphic Organizers 20
      Semantic Mapping 22

CONCLUSION 23

BIBLIOGRAPHY 24

The Author

Judith L. Irvin is Director, Center for the Study of Middle Level Education, Florida State University, College of Education, Department of Educational Leadership, Tallahassee.

The Advisory Panel

Ronald Barron, English Teacher, Richfield High School, Minnesota

Michael H. Jessup, Professor of Education, Towson State University, Maryland

Virginia Magnus, English Teacher, Northern Burlington County Regional High School, Columbus, New Jersey

Sue Peterson, Reading/ESL Specialist, Neenah Public Schools, Wisconsin

John W. Taylor, Associate Professor of English Linguistics, South Dakota State University, Brookings

INTRODUCTION

Clarke reads a story for his teacher about a canary in a space station; Claribel, the canary, is the central figure in the story. Although Clarke is reading about peeps and whistles, yellow feathers, and beaks, he cannot say "canary" the first three times he encounters the word. After two pages and much struggling, he tries again, saying "creature." Three paragraphs later when he meets "canary" again, he says "carney... car... canary, there it is, that's it!" He puts it all together. He is able to "get" this word because it is a word in his listening and speaking vocabulary, because he is able to depend on his knowledge of initial sound, and because he continues to put the context clues together to guess at the word.

Sounding out words and context clues would have been useless to Clarke if he had been attempting a word unknown to him. Pronouncing an unfamiliar word does not help a reader understand the text; furthermore, most contexts in natural text do not provide enough information to help the reader understand an unknown word; even looking up the word in the dictionary does not always help.

If the word "canary" appeared in a story about an aviary and the bird was not the central character, it would not be important for Clarke to "get" the word. All words are not created equal: some are more important in different contexts than others. Some are more or less known to students, some lend themselves to instruction and others do not, and some are contained in contextually rich environments and some are not.

Vocabulary knowledge has been under investigation for many years, but only in the last decade has solid research helped educators understand the factors in vocabulary acquisition and recommend instructional strategies that facilitate meaningful vocabulary learning. Guidance for vocabulary instruction has come only in the last decade because researchers needed to view vocabulary acquisition within the broader context of language learning. Educators now understand that vocabulary development is more than looking up words in a dictionary and writing sentences: it involves the complex process of relating words to ideas.

This monograph reviews the recent research on vocabulary knowledge. After a discussion of the importance of vocabulary knowledge, it examines the various factors in vocabulary acquisition identified by researchers in the last decade. It also includes a discussion of the issues related to vocabulary instruction and presents four guidelines for instruction. Finally, it describes researched and field-tested learning strategies designed to facilitate meaningful vocabulary learning.

A REVIEW OF THE RESEARCH
The Importance of Vocabulary Knowledge

A wealth of research documents the strong relationship between vocabulary knowledge and academic achievement, specifically reading and listening comprehension. Anderson and Freebody hypothesize that vocabulary knowledge is strongly related to comprehension because (a) understanding words enables readers to understand passages, and/or (b) verbal aptitude underlies both word and passage comprehension, and/or (c) vocabulary knowledge may be related to a person's store of background information (4).* Whatever the reason, we know that the proportion of difficult words in text is the single most powerful predictor of text difficulty, and a reader's general vocabulary knowledge is the single best predictor of how well that reader can understand text (4, 129). More simply put, "people who do not know the meanings of many words are probably poor readers" (4).

Nagy and Herman estimated that for students in grades four through twelve, a 4,500-to 5,400-word gap existed between low- versus high-achieving students (132). Others found huge individual differences between high- and low-ability students (69, 71, 155, 158). Nagy and Herman found a 4,700-word difference in vocabulary knowledge between upper-and lower-class students and estimated that middle-class first graders know about 50 percent more words than do lower-class first graders (132). The findings are clear: high-achieving students know more words than low-achieving students.

Until about 1950, vocabulary research focused on four areas: (a) vocabulary size at various ages, (b) the relationship between vocabulary and intelligence, (c) identifying the most useful words to know, and (d) identifying a core of words that make text more understandable. In sum, most of the early research centered on the choice of words to teach beginning readers and the implementation of readability formulas in the attempt to control text difficulty. Johnson predicted that the 1980s would be characterized as a period of the rediscovery of the importance of vocabulary instruction to reading comprehension: the promise was fulfilled (87).

The last 15 years have yielded much quality research in language comprehension and production. It is only within the context of this

---

*Numbers in parentheses appearing in the text refer to the Bibliography beginning on page 24.

research base that researchers and practitioners can understand vocabulary acquisition and make viable recommendations for effective instructional practices. Beck and McKeown contended that those interested in vocabulary acquisition must first understand the relationship between words and ideas, the role of inference, and the organization of information (13). It seems that previous attempts to study vocabulary acquisition were fruitless until researchers were able to reach at least some level of understanding of the complexities of the mental processes involved in relating words to ideas.

Factors in Vocabulary Acquisition

Chall estimated that typical first graders understand and use about 6,000 different words (30). Most primary students understand thousands more words than they recognize in print; nearly all these words represent concrete objects.

A shift in children's language takes place around age 10. The words they meet with increasing frequency thereafter are abstract rather than concrete; they encounter concepts in social studies texts, abstractions in stories, and specialized content words in science. The primary grades, then, can be characterized as a time to master "word recognition," whereas the intermediate grades and beyond may be the time to begin to meet the challenge of "word meanings" (30).

Although the research of the last two decades has helped to illuminate the complexity of the role of vocabulary instruction, it has left the resolution less clear. The first step in making decisions about effective vocabulary instruction is an understanding of various factors in vocabulary acquisition, including (a) what it means to "know" a word, (b) the role of context in incidental word learning, (c) the usefulness of definitions, and (d) the size and growth of vocabulary as a student matures.

Knowing Words

Beck, McKeown, McCaslin, and Burkes identified three levels of word knowledge: unknown, acquainted, and established (15). For example, if you ask a young child about different ways of measuring things in your home, you might mention a "gauge," which the child does not recognize (unknown). She recognizes "yardstick" as something to do with measuring, but would not be able to hand you one (acquainted); however she has used a "ruler" in the past to measure her foot (established). Nagy contends that it takes more than a simple, superficial knowledge of words to make a difference in reading comprehension (128). That is, readers do not need to know all words in text at the "established" level to comprehend what they are reading, but, for instruction of specific words to make an impact on reading comprehension, the understanding must be beyond a superficial level.

Blachowicz suggested the use of knowledge rating before reading to help students analyze their level of word knowledge (19). Before students read, the teacher presents a list of words related to the topic of study. The students then analyze what they know about each word individually and then discuss which words are hardest, or easiest, and share information. This activity leads naturally to the preteaching of vocabulary.

An issue related to knowing words is the importance of words in the text. Apparently students do not need to know all the words in a text to understand it. Freebody and Anderson found that replacing one content word in six with a difficult synonym did not reliably decrease sixth graders' comprehension of text (61). Generally, students encounter text with 3 to 6 percent unfamiliar words. In sum, if the unfamiliar words are not important to the understanding of the text, students can tolerate a fairly large number of unknown words (about 15 percent) and still read with comprehension.

Context

Few would dispute the value of students learning to use context to understand text and improve vocabulary growth. In light of recent research, however, a few caveats are warranted. In fact, Nagy maintained that "context, used as an instructional method by itself, is ineffective as a means of teaching new meanings, at least when compared with other forms of vocabulary instruction" (129, p. 7). He contended that context rarely provides enough information for the person who has no other knowledge about the word. In another study, Nagy calculated that the probability of learning a word from a single encounter (in context) was between .05 and .11 with seventh and eighth graders (128). Herman, Anderson, Pearson, and Nagy found that learning from context was facilitated by higher reading ability and by explicit text (81). The authors of these and other studies concluded that some learning from context occurs, but the effect is not very powerful.

One reason that context alone does not have powerful effects on vocabulary growth is that most contexts in natural text are relatively uninformative. Schatz and Baldwin found that such context offered no assistance in inferring the meanings of words for eleventh and twelfth graders (153). For a typical contrast-type context clue, such as "While Mary was sad, Mark was ecstatic," a number of meanings could be construed. A reader could substitute "unconcerned," "helpless," or even "morose." Further, writing sentences, a common practice in classrooms, should be questioned. Some students have mastered the "three-to-five-word sentence" in completing these assignments. For example, "She was energetic." "I live in a country." The sentences are correct, but they add nothing to the student's understanding of the word because a myriad of words could be substituted after the verb. Nagy warned that "a good context might help a student figure out the meaning of a less familiar synonym for a known word, but a single context is generally not adequate for teaching a new concept" (129, p.8).

Even considering these limitations, experts in vocabulary acquisition contend that the use of strategies to maximize the use of context, even if the context is lacking richness, is still useful instructional practice, especially when paired with other learning strategies. After considering the dilemma, Nagy maintained that a combination of definitional and contextual approaches is more effective than either approach alone (129).

Definitions

By itself, the activity of looking up words in a dictionary or committing definitions to memory does not lead to improved comprehension. This daily occurrence in hundreds of classrooms leads to only a superficial understanding and a rapid forgetting of a word. There are two problems with using definitions to learn new words: (a) often a person must know a word to understand the definition, and (b) definitions do not always contain enough information for understanding and using a word. For example, a student finding "trade" as a definition for the word "commerce" is likely to write a sentence such as, "I will commerce my baseball for your goalie shirt." In other words, reading comprehension depends on a deep understanding of the intent of the text, not merely on the definitional knowledge of the words.

Educators need to understand that learning a word involves more than lifting its meaning from context or reading its meaning in a dictionary. In fact, word knowledge involves a complex process of integrating new words with ideas that exist in the schema of the reader. Before an extensive discussion of vocabulary instruction with specific teaching suggestions, one last factor in the vocabulary acquisition process is also important to understand—the size and growth of vocabulary.

Size and Growth of Vocabulary

This has been a topic of long-standing debate. The number of words a person knows at any particular age depends on what an investigator counts as a word, with or without derivatives, and at what level a word is "known." General consensus and the most recent study (72) estimate that five to six year olds know between 2,500 and 5,000 words. Nagy and Herman estimate that students learn approximately 2,700 to 3,000 new words annually (133). Using a procedure called "fact mapping," Carey determined that school-aged children become aware of about seven new words each day but these words may not be retained or used after the initial exposure (23).

A factor related to the size and growth of vocabulary involves the number of words available for exposure. Analyzing the stock of words in school-printed material in grades 3 through 9, Nagy and Herman found that materials available for those grade levels contained approximately 88,500 words with upwards of 100,000 distinct meanings (133). Anderson and Freebody indicated that an average fifth grader would be likely to encounter almost 10,000 new words a year while completing normal school reading assignments (5).

Researchers have helped us understand that most children are capable of learning large numbers of new words each year. The question is—where and how do students learn these words? Durkin spent almost 300 hours observing fourth through sixth graders and found that only 19 minutes of instructional time was spent in direct vocabulary instruction (53). Also, Nagy, Herman, and Anderson, analyzing the number of words suggested in basal and content area textbook teacher's guides, determined that only 290–460 of the 3,000 words that students learn each year can be attributed to direct instruction (134). Nagy and Herman concluded that "teaching children specific words will not in itself contribute substantially to the overall size of their vocabulary" (p. 133, p. 23).

Although agreement is not universal, Nagy and Herman held "that incidental learning of words from context while reading is, or can be, the major mode of vocabulary growth once children have really begun to read" (133, p. 24). They based their belief on previous studies (81, 133) indicating that reading grade-level texts does produce a small, but statistically reliable, increase in word knowledge in the grades (3, 5, 7, 8) that were tested. The chance of learning a word from one exposure in text is about 1 in 20. These researchers concluded, however, that "if students were to spend 25 minutes a day reading at a rate of 200 words per minute for 200 days out of the year, they would read a million words of text annually'' (133, p. 26). With this amount of reading, students would encounter between 15,000 and 30,000 unfamiliar words and if they learned 1 in 20 of these words, their yearly gain in vocabulary would be between 750 and 1,500 words.

As Nagy pointed out, very few people have experienced systematic, intensive, and prolonged vocabulary instruction, yet many adults have acquired an extensive reading vocabulary (129). People learn words from a number of sources, but "after third grade, for those children who do read a reasonable amount, reading may be the single largest source of vocabulary growth'' (p. 30). In fact, Fielding, Wilson, and Anderson found that the amount of free reading was the best predictor of vocabulary growth between grades two and five (58).

ISSUES RELATED TO VOCABULARY INSTRUCTION

As previously stated, Nagy and Herman concluded that students can and do learn new words from context and that the number of words learned thereby is significantly greater than the number learned from direct instrucion (132). While few educators would dispute the value of reading, Jenkins, Stein, and Wysocki argued that incidental learning of vocabulary is not, necessarily, a by-product of wide reading (86). In a series of studies, Beck and McKeown and others found that (a) direct vocabulary instruction can increase comprehension if the text contains the words taught, (b) vocabulary instruction needs to be extensive and include frequent encounters with the word to effect comprehension, (c) instruction in vocabulary should include associating new words outside class, and (d) instruction can be most effective when words are related to each other meaningfully (17, 120, 121).

Marzano and Marzano summarized the research of vocabulary instruction as follows:

> Direct instruction increases knowledge of words taught. However, for instruction to transfer to reading, it must be relatively long in duration and foster a deep understanding of words . . . wide reading and language development activities must play a dominant role in vocabulary instruction. (115, p. 10)

According to this middle-ground position, wide reading should be the primary vehicle for vocabulary learning, yet some selected words can be the focus of direct vocabulary instruction. The natural assumption is that if this rich instruction focuses on helping students become independent word learners through morphemic analysis, contextual clues, and making the most of learning opportunities outside the classroom, then reading activities can be more effective.

Choosing Words for Instruction

Given that it is unlikely that students will learn a large number of words from direct instruction and given that instruction must be rich and extended to improve reading comprehension, even slightly, the words teachers choose for instruction are important.

Graves and Prenn classified words into three types, each requiring a higher investment of teacher and learner time for instruction (71). The first type is a word that is already in the student's oral vocabulary. Students merely need to identify the written symbol for such a word. These words are generally mastered by the fourth grade, but poor readers continue to have problems with them.

The second type of word is in neither the oral nor the reading vocabulary of the student, but it can be easily defined through the use of more familiar synonyms. For example, while a student may not know the meaning of the word "altercation," words such as "argument" or "quarrel" can easily help him/her to define it. Another type of word that fits into this category is a multiple-meaning word such as "bank," "run," or "bay." A student may know one meaning of such a word but need a new or second meaning explained. It is estimated that one-third of commonly used words have multiple meanings. These words are called *polysemous*.

Polysemous words may be historically related. For example, students may know that "coach" means someone who guides a team. They may not know, however, that a coach is also a vehicle. The new meaning can be traced to the term people in medieval England used to describe the person who guided a team of horses pulling a coach. The term was later applied to college tutors, leaders of crew teams, and even later to anyone who guided a team as hard to handle as eight spirited horses. Polysemous words may also have a specific meaning in a content area. For example, all students know the word "table." In math, however, "table" has a very specific meaning much different from its everyday meaning.

The third type of word is one for which the student has acquired no concept. It is encountered frequently in the content areas. Before students can understand the word, the teacher must take the time to develop the concept through instruction. Words such as "fission" or "valence" are difficult concepts that are more readily understood after examples are given. Nelson-Herber recognized the value of extensive reading to increase vocabulary knowledge, but maintained that "direct instruction that engages students in construction of word meaning, using context and prior knowledge, is effective for learning specific vocabulary and for improving comprehension of related materials" (136, p. 623). For these words that are difficult to teach and are commonly found in the content areas, rich, direct instruction is most helpful.

Words that are already in the student's listening vocabulary may be taught through Language Experience activities or other writing experiences; however, multiple-meaning words and those embodying unfamiliar concepts need more direct instruction. Words chosen for instruction should be considered important to the understanding of a particular content area or to enhance general background knowledge.

Elements of Effective Instruction

Although it is clear that increased vocabulary knowledge results in increased reading comprehension, how vocabulary instruction should be organized has been the subject of much debate in recent years. While the preteaching of vocabulary has been shown to increase scores on vocabulary tests, this instruction does not seem to improve scores on measures of general reading comprehension (86). Moore maintained that the relative importance of words to a passage determines their subsequent effect on comprehension (126). Other researchers have differentiated between the kinds of instruction given. Stahl and Fairbanks found that vocabulary instruction generally improves reading comprehension, but not all methods seem to have that effect (161). Vocabulary instruction that promotes student involvement seems to improve comprehension more than passive activities with words.

From the work of other researchers (67, 124, 161), Beck and McKeown concluded "that four statements about the effects of vocabulary instruction on word meaning can be made with a high degree of confidence: (a) all instructional methods produce better word learning than no instruction, (b) no one method has been shown to be consistently superior, (c) methods that use a variety of techniques seem to be advantageous, and (d) repeated exposures to chosen words for instruction aid in learning those words" (13).

What does this discussion of vocabulary instruction mean to the classroom teacher? Let's begin with what should *not* be done. "Word recognition instruction in which definitions are looked up in the dictionary or glossary and then used in a sentence is meaningless and often results in rote learning and rapid forgetting" (166, p. 603). This approach is a common way to teach vocabulary. The research clearly indicates, however, that this technique is also the least effective for the understanding and retention of words.

A synthesis of the research suggests that two guiding principles for effective vocabulary development are (a) to encourage wide reading and (b) to provide language-rich instructional activities. "Effective" may be defined as meaningful learning that attempts to relate new information to known information (166). Reviews of successful instructional practice (17, 124, 161) reveal that the direct instruction that is most likely to lead to improved reading comprehension has the following components: (a) multiple exposures to the word, (b) elaboration and discussion of word meanings connecting with students' prior knowledge to facilitate deep processing of words and their meanings (definitional and contextual meanings of words), and (c) application of word meanings to new situations. Beck and McKeown concluded that encouraging deep processing of words and the ideas that accompany them distinguishes instruction that improves comprehension from instruction that does not (13). A common thread running through such instructional practices is that these activities require students to use new information by comparing it with known information, thereby requiring them to construct their own word meanings.

GUIDELINES FOR INSTRUCTION

1. Help students become independent word learners. If educators accept the premise postulated by Nagy and others that wide reading is the most effective vehicle for large-scale vocabulary growth, then helping students make the most of learning words independently is imperative. Carr and Wixson (26) related this independence to the concept of strategic readers described by Paris, Lipson, and Wixson (138). They suggested that readers should be responsible for learning a variety of methods to acquire word meanings, have the ability to monitor their understanding of new vocabulary, and gain the capacity to change or modify strategies for understanding in the event of comprehension failure.

According to Nelson-Herber, "good teaching provides the learner with strategies not only for learning the task at hand, but for independent learning beyond the task at hand" (136, p. 629). Graphic organizers, mapping activities, the study of morphemics (structural analysis), and the use of context clues are ways that can help learners make the connection between new learning and existing learning, thus giving them more power to comprehend unfamiliar words in the future.

2. Encourage active involvement and deep processing of words. What students do with newly learned words is more important than the number of words presented. Teachers can help students associate new words with what they already know through meaningful content or known synonyms. Students can learn how to make associations on their own in order to relate new words to their existing knowledge. Using new associations in writing and speaking is helpful. Direct instruction that engages students in the construction of word meanings by using context and prior knowledge has been effective for learning specific vocabulary and important for the comprehension of related material (136).

For example, Beck and McKeown developed activities in which students described a situation involving a word—"Tell me about something you might want to *eavesdrop* on" or "Describe the most *melodious* sound you can think of" (12). When studying China, one teacher presented this question to her students: "Could a *nomad* be a *mandarin*?" She then asked students to match the following words by drawing lines:

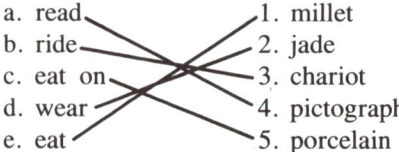

a. read   1. millet
b. ride   2. jade
c. eat on   3. chariot
d. wear   4. pictograph
e. eat   5. porcelain

3. Provide multiple exposure to words. The likelihood of a middle grade student acquiring an adult understanding of a word from one exposure in a natural context is very low (134). Many encounters with a new word are necessary if vocabulary instruction is to have a measurable effect on comprehension (122, 161). If words are to be retained, they must be used in meaningful ways in future reading and writing assignments. Logically, the introduction and use of new words should occur within a content area where reinforcement can naturally occur. An obvious cause-and-effect relationship is at work here: the more students are exposed to a word that occurs in a meaningful context, the higher their chance of using and understanding that word.

4. Help students develop a positive attitude about learning words outside the classroom. Activities and/or gimmicks that help students identify, say, hear, or see words studied in class help them experience repeated exposures in a meaningful context. The more curiosity about words students develop, the more likely they are to make vocabulary development a lifelong process. Word study in one subject and setting can and should be reinforced in other subjects and settings. Some teachers have found it motivational to have students bring in and share encounters with words they have studied previously. Additionally, these application exercises help students develop the attitude that increasing one's vocabulary is a lifelong process.

LEARNING STRATEGIES

The strategies that follow were chosen because they (a) help students become independent word learners; (b) encourage active involvement by having students relate new words to previously learned concepts; and (c) provide multiple exposures to new words through reading, writing, speaking, and listening activities.

List-Group-Label-Write

Taba first developed the List-Group-Label strategy as part of her Concept Development Model (165). This strategy can also be used as a diagnostic instrument to determine what students know about a subject and as an organizational tool to facilitate higher-level thinking. Since it involves the categorization and labeling of words, List-Group-Label makes an excellent prereading strategy for vocabulary development lessons as well.

Step 1: The teacher elicits from students as many words as possible related to a particular subject. The teacher may use a variety of stimuli: exhibiting a picture, reading a story, showing a film, or giving a lecture. Historical pictures of a city (such as Washington, D.C., in the late 1800s) may evoke responses such as horses, dirt roads, umbrellas. Words may also be elicited by simply asking students to brainstorm what they know about a particular topic.

Step 2: The teacher helps students group related items. Students determine appropriate categories and group the words accordingly. One type of marking system (for historical pictures of Washington, D.C.) is shown in Figure 1.

Step 3: The teacher helps students give a label to each group. After students have grouped related items, the teacher asks them to label each group of related words, using other words, signs, or symbols.

Taba's model extends this initial phase of categorizing into Interpretation of Data. To encourage students to think at higher levels, they would be asked to compare observations of old Washington with pictures of the city as it is today. They could then be asked to identify similarities and differences in the pictures. Further, students would be asked to make generalizations concerning the similarities and differences noted. In the Application of Generalization phase, students would apply the generalization to a new situation and examine what would happen if the generalization were applied. To continue our example, after the List-Group-Label

**Figure 1
Sample Marking System**

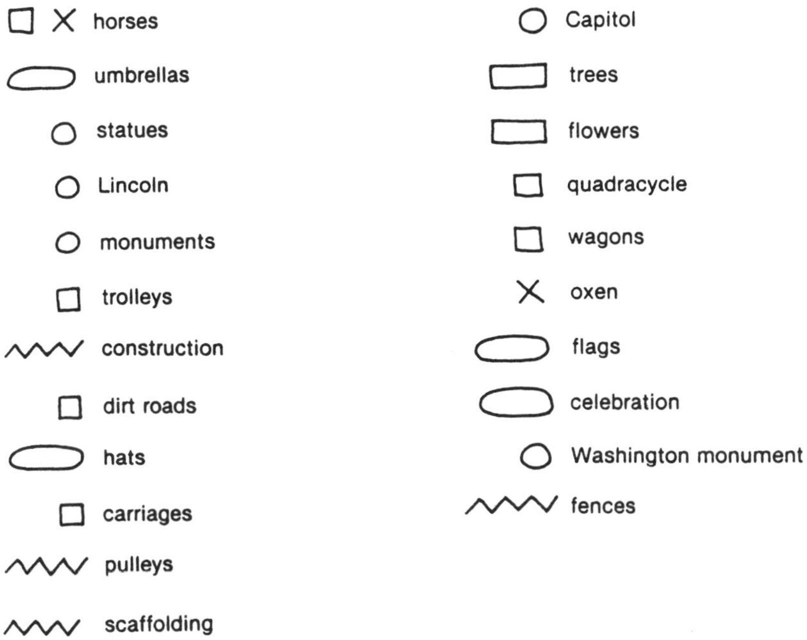

☐ ✗ horses
⬭ umbrellas
○ statues
○ Lincoln
○ monuments
☐ trolleys
∿ construction
☐ dirt roads
⬭ hats
☐ carriages
∿ pulleys
∿ scaffolding

○ Capitol
☐ trees
☐ flowers
☐ quadracycle
☐ wagons
✗ oxen
⬭ flags
⬭ celebration
○ Washington monument
∿ fences

activity about Washington, D.C., students may form the generalization that "Transportation has changed due to advances in technology." Then they may be asked to apply this same statement to a new situation by considering the question, "How will transportation change in the next 100 years?"

Educators have used the Taba Model as a means of promoting higher-level thinking and developing vocabulary knowledge in young students for two decades. This activity provides motivation through opportunity for success. All students can participate by sharing with the class their individual perceptions of a picture. They can then develop their higher-order thinking skills through categorizing, interpreting, and making generalizations. In addition, students learn words by grouping them logically and in a way that makes sense to them.

Semantic Feature Analysis

Johnson and Pearson developed this strategy to acquaint students with the notion that synonyms are never the "same as," but rather they are "something like" another word (91, 92). Through this procedure, students have the opportunity to make fine discriminations among word concepts. When using the strategy with general vocabulary, they learn the different connotations of words and better understand semantic relationships. This strategy also activates students' prior knowledge.

If Semantic Feature Analysis is used with technical vocabulary, students can discriminate between related concepts. An example from a United States history lesson illustrates the steps involved.

Step 1: The teacher selects a category. The category should consist of two or more items that are similar. For example, the teacher may select treaties and alliances between countries.

Step 2: The teacher lists related terms of the category. The teacher places the related terms along the left side of the page, blackboard, or transparency.

Step 3: The teacher then lists features to be emphasized. The features used to describe the terms are placed across the top of the page, blackboard, or transparency, as shown in Figure 2.

Step 4: Students complete the chart of the terms and features with teacher guidance. A "+" in the appropriate column indicates a positive relationship, a "-" a negative relationship, a "0" no relationship, and a "?" no consensus can be reached without further information. This part of the activity can be completed by small groups or the whole class.

Step 5: Students and teacher explore the matrix, making observations about it. The teacher may need to ask questions that elicit generalizations.

After conducting numerous research studies using Semantic Feature Analysis, Anders and Bos have concluded that this strategy "enables students to learn relationships between and among the conceptual vocabulary and the major ideas in the text" (2, p. 611).

Graphic Organizers

Originally called Structured Overviews by Ausubel (7), graphic organizers have been used as pre- and post-reading aids, as study strategies, and as vocabulary development activities. They are a way to show relationships between words in the form of a tree diagram. An example of a graphic organizer of the three types or words discussed on pages 12-13 is shown in Figure 3.

**Figure 2
Semantic Feature Analysis:
Indicating Relationships**

	Formal Agreement	Make Peace	More than Two Parties
alliance	+	?	?
treaty	+	+	0
affiliation	0	0	0
association	0	0	0
coalition	?	0	?
confederation	+	0	+
league	+	0	+

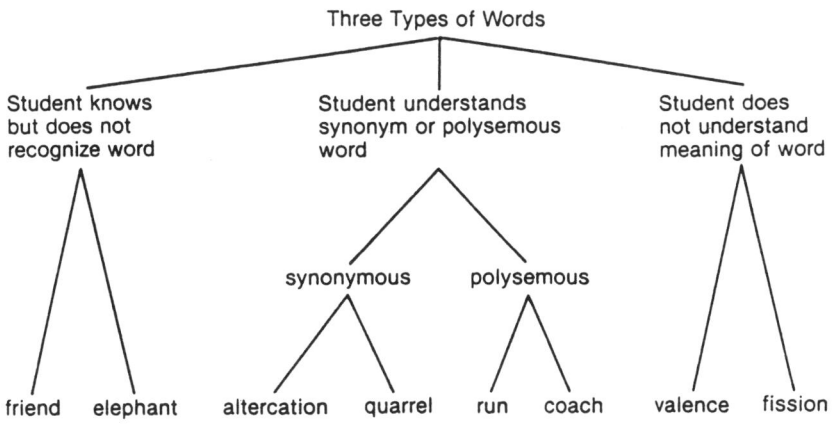

**Figure 3
Three Types of Words**

Moore and Readence reviewed the research on graphic organizers and drew four major conclusions (127). First, graphic organizers affect vocabulary test scores to a moderate degree. Students who used them tended to score slightly higher. Second, the maturity of the learner may influence the effectiveness of the organizer. That is, older students may benefit more from involvement with a graphic organizer than younger ones. Third, students who produce a graphic organizer after content is presented do better than those who only interact with organizers before content is presented. The amount of learner involvement seems to be a significant factor in the effectiveness of the organizers. Fourth, teachers who led students through graphic organizers seemed to perceive themselves as better prepared and more confident.

Graphic organizers are generally thought to be an effective way to introduce new vocabulary before reading. Some teachers have found partially completed organizers to be helpful in assisting students as they read. By having such an organizer as a guide, students are better able to arrange information and vocabulary hierarchically. The completed organizer may function as a summary of the reading.

Semantic Mapping

Semantic maps are diagrams that help students see the relationship between words. Since it was first developed by Hanf (77) and expanded by Johnson and Pearson (91, 92), this strategy has been used effectively as a pre- and post-reading technique, a prewriting activity, a study skill strategy, and a vocabulary development strategy. Research seems to support its effectiveness over more traditional techniques (93, 97, 113, 142, 169). The following steps illustrate the use of semantic mapping as a vocabulary development strategy.

Step 1: The teacher selects an important word or topic. The word should be familiar enough to students that they can readily list a group of words that relate to it.

Step 2: The teacher writes the word on the chalkboard or overhead projector.

Step 3: The teacher encourages students to think of as many related words as possible. They can complete this step first individually and then as a group by sharing lists.

Step 4: Students and teacher then add labels to groups. Some teachers copy completed maps onto chart paper and keep these large-sized maps posted for the duration of a unit. As students learn new words or discover new relationships, they can add them to the chart using a different colored marker. The charts give students a concise overview of the key concepts within a unit and of how concepts are related. They also enable students to relate new words to those they already understand.

Because semantic mapping helps students see relationships between ideas and connect known information with new information, it is a valuable tool for developing their vocabulary and conceptual understanding.

CONCLUSION

Researchers in the last decade have helped to illuminate a direction for effective vocabulary development for students. Educators have recognized the important role of vocabulary knowledge in comprehending text for some time. Recent investigations in the richness of context in natural text, the usefulness of text, the level to which a person "knows" a word, and the size and growth of vocabulary have helped educators understand that the acquisition of a full, rich, and functional vocabulary involves the complex process of relating words to ideas.

Experts in the field of language development agree that the main vehicle for vocabulary instruction should be encouraging students to read widely. Selected words, however, should be chosen for extended, rich instruction. This instruction should focus on helping students become independent learners, encouraging them to become actively involved in the processing of selected words, providing multiple exposures to words, and guiding them to develop a positive attitude toward learning words outside the classroom. Research-based and field-tested learning strategies such as List-Group-Label-Write, Semantic Feature Analysis, Graphic Organizers, and Semantic Mapping are available for use by teachers at any level. Along with wide reading, these strategies help students learn unfamiliar words by associating words to be learned with ideas and words they know.

BIBLIOGRAPHY

1. Ames, W. S. "The Development of a Classification Scheme of Contextual Aids." *Reading Research Quarterly* 2 (1966-1967): 57-62.
2. Anders, P. L., and Bos, C. S. "Semantic Feature Analysis: An Interactive Strategy for Vocabulary Development and Text Comprehension." *Journal of Reading* 29 (1986): 610-16.
3. Anders P.; Bos, C., and Filip, D. "The Effect of Semantic Feature Analysis on the Reading Comprehension of Learning-Disabled Students." In *Changing Perspectives on Research in Reading /Language Processing and Instruction*, edited by J. A. Niles and L. A. Harris. Rochester, N.Y.: National Reading Conference, 1984.
4. Anderson, R. C., and Freebody, P. "Vocabulary Knowledge." In *Comprehension and Teaching: Research Reviews*, edited by J. T. Guthrie. Newark, Del. International Reading Association, 1981.
5. ____. "Reading Comprehension and the Assessment and Acquisition of Word Knowledge." In *Advances in Reading/Language Research: A Research Annual*, edited by B. Hutton. Greenwich, Conn.: JAI Press, 1983.
6. Artley, A. S. "Teaching Word-Meaning Through Context." *Elementary English Review* 20 (1943): 68-74.
7. Ausubel, D. R. *Educational Psychology: A Cognitive View*. New York: Holt, Rinehart and Winston, 1968.
8. Barron, R. F. "The Use of Vocabulary as an Advance Organizer." In *Research in Reading in the Content Areas: First Year Report*, edited by H. L. Herber, and P. L. Sanders. Syracuse, N.Y.: Syracuse University Reading and Language Arts Center, 1969.
9. Bean, T. W.; Singer, H.; and Cowan, S. "Analogical Study Guides: Improving Comprehension in Science." *Journal of Reading* 29 (1985): 246-50.
10. Beck, I. "Developing Comprehension: The Impact of the Directed Reading Lesson." In *Learning to Read in American Schools: Basal Readers and Content Text*, edited by R. C. Anderson, J. Osborn, and R. J. Tierney. Hillsdale, N. J.: Erlbaum, 1984.
11. Beck, I.; McCaslin, M.; and McKeown, M. *The Rationale and Design of a Program to Teach Vocabulary to Fourth Grade Students*. Pittsburgh, Penn.: University of Pittsburgh, Learning Research and Development Center, 1980.
12. Beck, I. L., and McKeown, M. G. "Learning Words Well—A Program to Enhance Vocabulary and Comprehension." *Reading Teacher* 36 (1983): 622.
13. ____. "The Acquisition of Vocabulary." In *Handbook of Reading Research*, edited by P. D. Pearson. 2d ed. White Plains, N.Y.: Longman, 1990.
14. Beck, I.; McKeown, M.; and McCaslin, E. "All Contexts Are Not Created Equal." *Elementary School Journal* 83 (1983): 177-81.
15. Beck, I. L.; McKeown, M. G.; McCaslin, E. S.; and Burkes, A. M. *Instructional Dimensions That May Affect Reading Comprehension: Examples from Two Commercial Reading Programs*. Pittsburgh, Penn.: University of Pittsburgh, Learning Research and Development Center, 1979.
16. Beck, I. L.; McKeown, M. G.; and Omanson, R. "The Effects and Uses of Diverse Vocabulary Instructional Techniques." In *The Nature of Vocabulary Acquisition*, edited by M. McKeown, and M. Curtis. Hillsdale, N. J.: Erlbaum, 1987.
17. Beck, I. L.; Perfetti, C. A.; and McKeown, M. G. "The Effects of Long-Term Vocabulary Instruction on Lexical Access and Reading Comprehension." *Journal of Educational Psychology* 74 (1982): 506-21.

18. Blachowicz, C. L. "Vocabulary Development and Reading: From Research to Instruction." *Reading Teacher* 38 (1985): 876-81.
19. ____. "Making Connections: Alternatives to the Vocabulary Notebook." *Journal of Reading* 29 (1986): 643-49.
20. ____. "Vocabulary Instruction: What Goes On in the Classroom?" *Reading Teacher* 41 (1987): 132-37.
21. Bromley, K. D. "Precis Writing: Promoting Vocabulary Development and Comprehension." In *Classroom Strategies for Secondary Reading*, edited by W. J. Harker. Newark, Del.: International Reading Association, 1985.
22. Bruck, M. "The Word Recognition and Spelling of Dyslexic Children." *Reading Research Quarterly* 23 (1988): 51-69.
23. Carey, S. "The Child as Word Learner." In *Linguistic Theory and Psychological Reality*, edited by M. Halle, J. Bresman, and G. Miller. Cambridge, Mass.: MIT Press, 1978.
24. Carnine, D.; Kameenui, E. J.; and Coyle, G. "Utilization of Contextual Information in Determining the Meaning of Unfamiliar Words in Context." *Reading Research Quarterly* 19 (1984): 188-202.
25. Carr, E. M. "The Vocabulary Overview Guide: A Metacognitive Strategy to Improve Vocabulary Comprehension and Retention." *Journal of Reading* 28 (1985): 684-89.
26. Carr, E. M., and Wixson, K. K. "Guidelines for Evaluating Vocabulary Instruction." *Journal of Reading* 29 (1986): 588-95.
27. Carroll, B., and Drum, P. A. "Definitional Games for Explicit and Implicit Context Clues." In *The Nature of Intelligence*, edited by J. A. Niles, and L. A. Harris. Hillsdale, N. J.: Erlbaum, 1983.
28. Carroll, J. B.; Davies, P.; and Richman, B. *Word Frequency Book*. New York: American Heritage, 1971.
29. Ceprano, M. A. "A Review of Selected Research on Methods of Teaching Sight Words." *Reading Teacher* 35 (1981): 314.
30. Chall, J. S. "Two Vocabularies for Reading: Recognition and Meaning." In *The Nature of Vocabulary Acquisition*, edited by M. G. McKeown, and M. E. Curtis. Hillsdale, N. J.: Erlbaum, 1987.
31. Clifford, G. J. "Words for Schools: The Applications in Education of the Vocabulary Research of Edward L. Thorndike." In *Impact of Research on Education: Some Case Studies*, edited by P. Suppes. Washington, D. C.: National Academy of Education, 1978.
32. Craik, F. I., and Tulving, E. "Depth of Processing and Retention of Words in Episodic Memory." *Journal of Experimental Psychology* 104 (1975): 268-94.
33. Crist, R. L., and Petrone, J. M. "Learning Concepts from Contexts and Definitions." *Journal of Reading Behavior* 9 (1977): 301-3.
34. Cronbach, L. J. "An Analysis of Techniques for Systematic Vocabulary Testing." *Journal of Educational Research* 36 (1942): 206-17.
35. ____. "Measuring Knowledge of Precise Word Meaning." *Journal of Educational Research* 36 (1943): 528-34.
36. Curtis, M. E. "Vocabulary Testing and Instruction." In *The Nature of Vocabulary Acquisition*, edited by M. G. McKeown, and M. E. Curtis. Hillsdale, N. J.: Erlbaum, 1987.
37. Curtis, R. V., and Reigeluth, C. M. "The Use of Analogies in Written Text." *Instructional Science* 13 (1984): 99-117.
38. Dale, E. "The Problem of Vocabulary in Reading." *Educational Research Bulletin* 25 (1956): 113-23.

39. _____. "Vocabulary Measurement: Techniques and Major Findings." *Elementary English* 45 (1965): 895-901, 948.
40. Dale, E.; O'Rourke, J.; and Bamman, H. A. *Techniques of Teaching Vocabulary*. Menlo Park, Calif.: Field Educational Publications, 1971.
41. Dale, E., and Razik, T. *Bibliography of Vocabulary Studies*. Columbus, Ohio: Ohio State University, Bureau of Educational Research and Service, 1963.
42. Davison, A., and Kantor, R. "On the Failure of Readability Formulas to Define Readable Texts: A Case Study from Adaptations." *Reading Research Quarterly* 17 (1982): 187-210.
43. Deighton, D. *Vocabulary Development in the Classroom*. New York: Bureau of Publications, Teachers College, Columbia University, 1959.
44. Dolch, E. W. *Reading and Word Meanings*. New York: Ginn, 1932.
45. _____. "How Much Word Knowledge Do Children Bring to Grade 1?" *Elementary English Review* 13 (1936): 177-83.
46. Dolch, E. W., and Leeds, D. "Vocabulary Tests and Depth of Meaning." *Journal of Educational Research* 47 (1953): 181-89.
47. Draper, A. G., and Moeller, G. H. "We Think with Words (Therefore, To Improve Thinking, Teach Vocabulary)." *Phi Delta Kappan* 52 (1971): 482-84.
48. Drum, P. A. "Vocabulary Knowledge." In *Searches for Meaning in Reading/Language Processes and Instruction*, edited by J. A. Niles and L. A. Harris. Rochester, N. Y.: National Reading Conference, 1983.
49. Drum, P. A., and Konopak, B. "Learning Word Meanings from Written Context." In *The Nature of Vocabulary Acquisition*, edited by M. McKeown and M. Curtis. Hillsdale, N. J.: Erlbaum, 1987.
50. Duffelmeyer, F. A. "The Effect of Context Clues on the Vocabulary Test Performance of Word Dominant and Paragraph Dominant Readers." *Journal of Reading* 27 (1984): 508-13.
51. Duin, A., and Graves, M. "Intensive Vocabulary Instruction: A Prewriting Technique." *Reading Research Quarterly* 22 (1987): 311-30.
52. Dulin, K. "New Research of Context Clues." *Journal of Reading* 12 (1970): 33-38.
53. Durkin, D. "What Classroom Observations Reveal About Reading Comprehension Instruction." *Reading Research Quarterly* 14 (1978-1979): 481-533.
54. Elivian, J. "Word Perception and Word Meaning in Student Reading in the Intermediate Grades." *Education* 59 (1938): 51-56.
55. Elshout-Mohr, M., and van Daalen-Kapteijns, M. M. "Cognitive Processes in Learning Word Meanings." In *The Nature of Vocabulary Acquisition*, edited by M. G. McKeown, and M. E. Curtis. Hillsdale, N. J.: Erlbaum, 1987.
56. Emans, R. "Teaching the Use of Context Clues." *Elementary English* 44 (1967): 243-46.
57. Feifel, H., and Lorge, I. "Qualitative Differences in the Vocabulary Responses of Children." *Journal of Educational Psychology* 41 (1950): 1-18.
58. Fielding, L. G.; Wilson, P. T.; and Anderson, R. C. "A New Focus on Free Reading: The Roles of Trade Books in Reading Instruction." In *The Contexts of School-Based Literacy*, edited by T. Raphael. New York: Random House, 1986.
59. Finn, P. J. "Word Frequency, Information Theory, and Cloze Performance: A Transfer Theory of Processing in Reading." *Reading Research Quarterly* 13 (1977-1978): 508-37.

60. Freebody, P., and Anderson, R. C. "Effects of Vocabulary Difficulty, Text Cohesion, and Schema Availability on Reading Comprehension." Urbana, Ill.: Center for the Study of Reading, 1981. ED 212 987.
61. _____. "Effects of Text Comprehension of Different Proportions and Locations of Difficult Vocabulary." *Journal of Reading Behavior* 15 (1983): 19-39.
62. Gipe, J. P. "Investigating Techniques for Teaching Word Meanings." *Reading Research Quarterly* 14 (1978-1979): 624-44.
63. _____. "Use of Relevant Context Helps Kids Learn New Word Meanings." *Reading Teacher* 33 (1980): 398-402.
64. Gold, P. C. "Two Strategies for Reinforcing Sight Vocabulary of Language Experience Stories." *Reading Teacher* 35 (1981): 141.
65. Gough, P. B. "Word Recognition." In *Handbook of Reading Research*, edited by P. D. Pearson. New York: Longman, 1984.
66. Graves, M. F. "Selecting Vocabulary to Teach in the Intermediate and Secondary Grades." In *Promoting Reading Comprehension*, edited by J. Flood. Newark, Del.: International Reading Association, 1984.
67. _____. "Vocabulary Learning and Instruction." *Review of Research in Education* 13 (1986): 91-128.
68. _____. "The Roles of Instruction in Fostering Vocabulary Development." In *The Nature of Vocabulary Acquisition*, edited by M. G. McKeown, and M. E. Curtis. Hillsdale, N. J.: Erlbaum, 1987.
69. Graves, M. F.; Brunetti, G. J.; and Slater, W. H. "The Reading Vocabularies of Primary Grade Children of Varying Geographic and Social Backgrounds." In *New Inquiries in Reading Research and Instruction*, edited by J. A. Harris and L. A. Harris. Rochester, N. Y.: National Reading Conference, 1982.
70. Graves, M. F., and Duin, A. L. "Building Students' Expressive Vocabularies." *Educational Perspectives* 23 (1985): 4-10.
71. Graves, M. F., and Prenn, M. C. "Costs and Benefits of Various Methods of Teaching Vocabulary." *Journal of Reading* 29 (1986): 596-602.
72. Graves, M. F., and Slater, W. H. "The Development of Reading Vocabularies in Rural Disadvantaged Students, Inner-City Disadvantaged Students, and Middle-Class Suburban Students." Paper presented at the meeting of the American Educational Research Association, Washington, D.C., 1987.
73. Gray, W., and Holmes, E. *The Development of Meaning Vocabularies in Reading*. Chicago: University of Chicago Press, 1938.
74. Hafner, L. E. "A One-Month Experiment in Teaching Context Aids in Fifth Grade." *Journal of Educational Research* 58 (1965): 471-74.
75. Haggard, M. R. "The Vocabulary Self-Collection Strategy: An Active Approach to Word Learning." *Journal of Reading* 26 (1982): 203-7.
76. _____. "The Vocabulary Self-Collection Strategy: Using Student Interest and World Knowledge to Enhance Vocabulary Growth." *Journal of Reading* 29 (1986): 634-42.
77. Hanf, M. B. "Mapping: A Technique for Translating Reading into Thinking." *Journal of Reading* 14 (1971): 225-30, 270.
78. Harris, A. J., and Jacobson, M. D. *Basic Elementary Reading Vocabularies*. New York: Macmillan, 1972.
79. Hayes, D. A., and Tierney, R. J. "Developing Readers' Knowledge Through Analogy." *Reading Research Quarterly* 17 (1982): 256-80.
80. Heimlich, J. E., and Pittleman, S. D. *Semantic Mapping: Classroom Applications*. Newark, Del.: International Reading Association, 1986.

81. Herman, P. A.; Anderson, R. C.; Pearson, P. D.; and Nagy W. "Incidental Acquisition of Word Meaning from Expositions with Varied Text Features." *Reading Research Quarterly* 22 (1987): 263-84.
82. Irvin, J. L. *Reading and the Middle School Student: Strategies to Enhance Literacy.* Needham Heights, Mass.: Allyn and Bacon, 1990.
83. Jackson, J. R., and Dizney, H. "Intensive Vocabulary Training." *Journal of Developmental Reading* 6 (1963): 221-29.
84. Jenkins, J. R., and Dixon, R. "Vocabulary Learning." *Contemporary Educational Psychology* 8 (1983): 237-60.
85. Jenkins, J. R.; Pany, D.; and Schreck, J. "Vocabulary and Reading Comprehension: Instructional Effects." Technical Report No. 100. Urbana Ill.: Center for the Study of Reading, 1978. ED 160 999.
86. Jenkins, J. R.; Stein, M.; and Wysocki, K. "Learning Vocabulary Through Reading." *American Educational Research Journal* 21 (1984): 767-87.
87. Johnson, D. D. "Introduction: Vocabulary." *Journal of Reading* 29 (1986): 580.
88. Johnson, D. D., and Bauman, J. F. "Word Identification." In *Handbook of Reading Research*, edited by P. D. Pearson. New York: Longman, 1984.
89. Johnson, D. D., and Johnson, B. Hott. "Highlighting Vocabulary in Inferential Comprehension Instruction. *Journal of Reading* 29 (1986). 622-26.
90. Johnson, D. D., and Majer E. "Johnson's Basic Vocabulary: Words for Grades 1 and 2." *Elementary School Journal* 77 (1976): 74-82.
91. Johnson, D. D., and Pearson, P. D. *Teaching Reading Vocabulary.* New York: Holt, Rinehart and Winston, 1978.
92. _____. *Teaching Reading Vocabulary.* 2d ed. New York: Holt, Rinehart and Winston, 1984.
93. Johnson, D. D.; Toms-Bronowski, S.; and Pittleman, S. D. "An Investigation of the Effectiveness of Semantic Mapping and Semantic Feature Analysis with Intermediate Grade Level Students." Program Report 83-3. Madison, Wis.: Wisconsin Center for Education Research, 1982.
94. Kameenui, E. J.; Carnine, D. W.; and Freschi, R. "Effects of Text Construction and Instructional Procedures for Teaching Word Meanings on Comprehension and Recall." *Reading Research Quarterly* 17 (1982): 367-88.
95. Kameenui, E. J.; Dixon, R. C.; and Carnine, D. W. "Issues in the Design of Vocabulary Instruction." In *The Nature of Vocabulary Acquisition*, edited by M. G. McKeown and M. E. Curtis. Hillsdale, N. J.: Erlbaum, 1987.
96. Kaplan, E. M., and Tuchman, A. "Vocabulary Strategies Belong in the Hands of Learners." In *Classroom Strategies for Secondary Reading*, edited by W. J. Harker. Newark, Del.: International Reading Association, 1985.
97. Karbon, J. C. "An Investigation of the Relationships Between Prior Knowledge and Vocabulary Development Using Semantic Mapping with Culturally Diverse Students." Doctoral dissertation, University of Wisconsin, Madison, 1984.
98. Kibby M. W. "A Note on the Relationship of Word Difficulty and Word Frequency." *Psychological Reports* 41 (1977): 12-14.
99. Kirkpatrick, E. A. "The Number of Words in an Ordinary Vocabulary." *Science* 18 (1891): 107-8.
100. Kirkpatrick, J. J., and Cureton, E. E. "Vocabulary Item Difficulty and Word Frequency." *Journal of Applied Psychology* 33 (1949): 347-51.
101. Kleiman, G. M. "The Effect of Previous Context on Reading Individual Words." Urbana, Ill.: Center for the Study of Reading, 1977. ED 134 941.

102. Klein, H.; Klein, G. A.; and Bertino, M. "Utilization of Context for Word Identification in Children." *Journal of Experimental Child Psychology* 17 (1974): 79–86.
103. Kruglov, L. P. "Qualitative Differences in the Vocabulary Choice of Children as Revealed in a Multiple-Choice Test." *Journal of Educational Psychology* 44 (1963): 229–43.
104. Kuczaj, S. A., II. "Acquisition of Word Meaning in the Context of the Development of the Semantic System." In *Verbal Processes in Children*, edited by C. J. Brainerd and M. Pressley. New York: Springer-Verlag, 1982.
105. Laffey, D. G., and Laffey, J. L. "Vocabulary Teaching: An Investment in Literacy." *Journal of Reading* 29 (1986): 650–56.
106. Levin, J. R.; Dretzke, B. J.; Pressley, M.; and McGivern, J. E. "In Search of the Keyword Method/Vocabulary Comprehension Link." *Contemporary Educational Psychology* 10 (1985): 220–27.
107. Levin, J. R.; Johnson, D. D.; Pittleman, S. D.; Levin, K. M.; Shriber, L. D.; Toms-Bronowski, S.; and Hayes, B. L. "A Comparison of Semantic- and Mnemonic-Based Vocabulary Learning Strategies." *Reading Psychology* 5 (1984): 1–16.
108. Levin, J. R., and Pressley, M. "Mnemonic Vocabulary Instruction: What's Fact, What's Fiction." In *Individual Differences in Cognition*, edited by R. F. Dillon. Orlando. Fla.: Academic Press, 1985.
109. Litowitz, B. "Learning to Make Definitions." *Journal of Child Language* 4 (1976): 289–304.
110. Loban, G. *The Language of Elementary School Children*. Champaign, Ill.: National Council of Teachers of English, 1963.
111. Lorge, I., and Chall, J. "Estimating the Size of Vocabularies of Children and Adults: An Analysis of Methodological Issues." *Journal of Experimental Education* 32 (1963): 147–57.
112. Madison, J.; Carroll, B.; and Drum, P. A. "The Effect of Directionality and Proximity of Context Clues on the Comprehension of Words." In *New Inquiries in Reading Research and Instruction*, edited by J. A. Niles and L. A. Harris. Rochester, N. Y.: National Reading Conference, 1982.
113. Margosein, C. M.; Pascarella, E. T.; and Pflaum, S. W. "The Effects of Instruction Using Semantic Mapping on Vocabulary and Comprehension." Paper presented at the meeting of the American Educational Research Association, New York, 1982. ED 217 390.
114. Marks, C. B.; Doctorow, M. J.; and Wittrock, M. C. "Word Frequency and Reading Comprehension." *Journal of Educational Research*, 67 (1974): 259–62.
115. Marzano. R. J., and Marzano, J. S. *A Cluster Approach to Elementary Vocabulary Instruction*. Newark, Del.: International Reading Association, 1988.
116. Mason, J. M.; Kniseley, E.; and Kendall, J. "Effects of Polysemous Words on Sentence Comprehension." *Reading Research Quarterly* 15 (1979): 49–65.
117. McCullough, C. M. "Learning to Use Context Clues." *Elementary English Review* 10 (1943): 140–43.
118. ———. "The Recognition of Context Clues in Reading." *Elementary English Review* 22 (1945): 1–5; 40.
119. ———. "Context Aids in Reading." *Reading Teacher* 11 (1958): 224–29.
120. McKeown, M. G. "The Acquisition of Word Meaning from Context by Children of High and Low Ability." *Reading Research Quarterly* 20 (1985): 482–96.
121. McKeown, M. G.; Beck, I. L.; Omanson, R. C.; and Perfetti, C. A. "The Effects of Long-Term Vocabulary Instruction on Reading Comprehension: A Replication." *Journal of Reading Behavior* 15 (1983): 3–18.
122. McKeown, M. G., Beck, I.; Omanson, R.; and Pople, M. "Some Effects of the

Nature and Frequency of Vocabulary Instruction on the Knowledge and Use of Words." *Reading Research Quarterly* 20 (1985): 222-35.

123. McKeown, M. G., and Curtis, M. E. *The Nature of Vocabulary Acquisition.* Hillsdale, N. J.: Erlbaum, 1987.

124. Mezynski, K. "Issues Concerning the Acquisition of Knowledge: Effects of Vocabulary Training on Reading Comprehension." *Review of Educational Research* 53 (1983): 253-79.

125. Miller, G., and Gildea, P. "How Children Learn Words." *Scientific American* 257 (1987): 94-99.

126. Moore, D. "Vocabulary." In *Research Within Reach: Secondary School Reading*, edited by D. Alvermann, D. Moore, and M. Conley. Newark, Del.: International Reading Association, 1987.

127. Moore, D. W., and Readence, J. E. "A Quantitative and Qualitative Review of Graphic Organizer Research." *Journal of Educational Research* 78 (1984): 11-17.

128. Nagy, W. E. "Vocabulary Instruction: Implications of the New Research." Paper presented at the meeting of the National Council of Teachers of English, Philadelphia, 1985.

129. _____. *Teaching Vocabulary to Improve Reading Comprehension.* Newark, Del.: International Reading Association, 1988.

130. Nagy, W. E., and Anderson, R. C. "How Many Words Are There in Printed School English?" *Reading Research Quarterly* 19 (1984): 304-30.

131. Nagy, W. E.; Anderson, R. C.; and Herman, P. A. "Learning Word Meanings from Context During Normal Reading." *American Educational Research Journal* 24 (1987): 237-70.

132. Nagy, W. E., and Herman, P. A. "Limitations of Vocabulary Instruction." Technical Report No. 326. Urbana, Ill.: Center for the Study of Reading, 1984. ED 248 498.

133. _____. "Breadth and Depth of Vocabulary Knowledge: Implications for Acquisition, and Instruction." In *The Nature of Vocabulary Acquisition*, edited by M. G. McKeown and M. E. Curtis. Hillsdale, N. J.: Erlbaum, 1987.

134. Nagy, W. E.; Herman, P. A.; and Anderson, R. C. "Learning Words from Context." *Reading Research Quarterly* 20 (1985); 233-53.

135. Nelson, K. "Cognitive Development and the Acquisition of Concepts." In *Schooling and the Acquisition of Knowledge*, edited by R. C. Anderson, R. J. Spiro, and W. E. Montague. Hillsdale, N. J.: Erlbaum, 1977.

136. Nelson-Herber, J. "Expanding and Refining Vocabulary in Content Areas." *Journal of Reading* 29 (1986): 626-33.

137. Pany, D.; Jenkins, J. R.; and Schreck, J. "Vocabulary Instruction: Effects on Word Knowledge and Reading Comprehension." *Learning Disabilities Quarterly* 5 (1982): 202-15.

138. Paris, S.; Lipson, M. Y.; and Wixson, K. K. "Becoming a Strategic Reader." *Contemporary Educational Psychology* 8 (1983): 293-316.

139. Patberg, J. A.; Graves, M. F.; and Stibbe, M. A. "Effects of Active Teaching and Practice in Facilitating Students' Use of Context Clues." In *Changing Perspectives on Reading/Language Processing and Instruction*, edited by J. A. Niles, and L. A. Harris. Rochester, N. Y.: National Reading Conference, 1984.

140. Pearson, P. D., and Studt, A. "Effects of Word Frequency and Contextual Richness on Children's Word Identification Abilities." *Journal of Educational Psychology* 67 (1975): 89-95.

141. Petty, W. T.; Herold, C. P.; and Stoll, E. *The State of Knowledge About the Teaching*

of Vocabulary. Champaign, Ill.: National Council of Teachers of English, 1986.

142. Pittleman, S. D.; Levin, K. M.; and Johnson, D. D. "An Investigation of Two Instructional Settings in the Use of Semantic Mapping with Poor Readers." Program Report 85-4. Madison, Wis.: Wisconsin Center for Education Research, 1985.

143. Pressley, M.; Levin, J.; and McDaniel, M. "Remembering Versus Inferring What a Word Means: Mnemonic and Contextual Approaches." In *The Nature of Vocabulary Acquisition*, edited by M. G. McKeown, and M. E. Curtis. Hillsdale, N. J.: Erlbaum, 1987.

144. Quealy, R. J. "Senior High School Students' Use of Context Aids in Reading." *Reading Research Quarterly* 4 (1969): 512-32.

145. Rankin, E. F., and Overholser, B. M. "Reaction of Intermediate Grade Children to Contextual Clues." *Journal of Reading Behavior* 1 (1969): 50-73.

146. Robinson, A. H. "A Study of Techniques of Word Identification." *Reading Teacher* 16 (1963): 238-42.

147. Roser, N., and Juel, C. "Effects of Vocabulary Instruction on Reading Comprehension." In *New Inquiries in Reading: Research and Instruction*, edited by J. Niles and L. A. Harris. Rochester, N. Y.: National Reading Conference, 1982.

148. Rubin, D. C. "The Effectiveness of Context Before, After, and Around a Missing Word." *Perception and Psychophysics* 19 (1976): 214-16.

149. Ruddell, R. B. "Vocabulary Learning: A Process Model and Criteria for Evaluating Instructional Strategies." *Journal of Reading* 29 (1986): 581-87.

150. Russell, D. H., and Saadeeh, I. Q. "Qualitative Levels in Children's Vocabularies." *Journal of Educational Psychology* 53 (1962): 170-74.

151. Sachs, H. "The Reading Method of Acquiring Vocabulary." *Journal of Educational Research* 36 (1943): 457-64.

152. Salus, P. H., and Salus, M. W. "Word Finding, Word Organizing, and Reading." In *Understanding Reading Comprehension: Cognition, Language, and the Structure of Prose*, edited by J. Flood. Newark, Del.: International Reading Association, 1984.

153. Schatz, E. K., and Baldwin, R. S. "Context Clues Are Unreliable Predictors of Word Meanings." *Reading Research Quarterly* 21 (1986): 429-53.

154. Schwartz, R. M., and Raphael, T. E. "Concept of Definition: A Key to Improving Students' Vocabulary." *Reading Teacher* 39 (1985): 198-205.

155. Seashore, R. H., and Eckerson, L. D. "The Measurement of Individual Differences in General English Vocabularies." *Journal of Educational Psychology* 31 (1940): 14-38.

156. Shibles, B. H. "How Many Words Does the First Grade Child Know?" *Elementary English* 31 (1959); 42-47.

157. Simpson, M. L. "Alternative Formats for Evaluating Content Area Vocabulary Understanding." *Journal of Reading* 31 (1987): 20-27.

158. Smith, M. K. "Measurement of the Size of General English Vocabulary Through the Elementary Grades and High School." *Genetic Psychological Monographs* 24 (1941): 311-45.

159. Stahl, S. A. "Differential Word Knowledge and Reading Comprehension." *Journal of Reading Behavior* 15 (1983): 33-50.

160. ———. "Three Principles of Effective Vocabulary Instruction." *Journal of Reading* 29 (1986): 662-68.

161. Stahl, S. A., and Fairbanks, M. M. "The Effects of Vocabulary Instruction: A Model-Based Meta-analysis." *Review of Educational Research* 56 (1986): 72-110.

162. Sternberg, R. "Most Vocabulary Is Learned from Context." In *The Nature of Vocabulary Acquisition*, edited by M. G. McKeown and M. E. Curtis. Hillsdale, N.J.:

Erlbaum, 1987.
163. Sternberg, R., and Powell, J. S. "Comprehending Verbal Comprehension." *American Psychologist* 38 (1983): 878–93.
164. Sternberg, R.; Powell, J. S.; and Kaye, D. B. "The Nature of Verbal Comprehension." In *Communicating with Computers in Classrooms: Prospects for Applied Cognitive Science*, edited by A. C. Wilkinson. New York: Academic Press, 1983.
165. Taba, H. *Teacher's Handbook for Elementary Social Studies*. Reading, Mass.: Addison-Wesley, 1967.
166. Thelen, J. N. "Vocabulary Instruction and Meaningful Learning." *Journal of Reading* 29 (1986): 603–9.
167. Thorndike, E. L. "Reading and Reasoning: A Study of Mistakes in Paragraph Reading." *Journal of Educational Psychology* 8 (1917): 323–32.
168. _____. *The Teacher's Word Book*. New York: Columbia University, Columbia University, Teachers College, 1921.
169. Toms-Bronowski, S. "An Investigation of the Effectiveness of Selected Vocabulary Teaching Strategies with Intermediate Grade Level Students." Doctoral dissertation, University of Wisconsin at Madison, 1983.
170. van Daalen-Kapteijns, M. M., and Elshout-Mo, M. "The Acquisition of Word Meaning as a Cognitive Learning Process." *Journal of Verbal Learning and Verbal Behavior* 20 (1981): 386–89.
171. Werner, H., and Kaplan, E. "The Acquisition of Word Meaning: A Developmental Study." *Monographs of the Society for Research in Child Development* 15 (1952).
172. Wesman, G. G., and Seashore, H. G. "Frequency vs. Complexity of Words in Verbal Measurement." *Journal of Educational Psychology* 40 (1949): 395–404.
173. Zakaluk, B. L.; Samuels, S. J.; and Taylor, B. M. "A Simple Technique for Estimating Prior Knowledge: Word Association." *Journal of Reading* 30 (1986): 56–60.